HANNIBAL AT THE DOOR

By

RICHARD GAREY

With Illustrations By

PATRICIA GAREY

Layout and Design By

SKYE CHILDERS

CONTENTS

PREFACE

In 2003 Patricia and I purchased a building on Main Street and moved to Hannibal, Missouri, boyhood home of Samuel Clemens. Over the years my work as an actor performing Mark Twain Himself and my renovation of three historic buildings has been personally transforming. This book grew out of our work on the John Robards Mansion on Sixth Street. I felt compelled to write it.

The project also owes much to my historic research and insight through Sam Clemens writings. Sam seemed to have ambivalent feelings about the town that inspired his greatest literary masterpieces. My book grew out of these eternal contradictions.

Hannibal attracts highly educated literary scholars from all over the world and often celebrates its rowdy frontier roots. Hannibalians embrace the arts and also love to hoot and holler and fire up the motorcycles. Hannibal is in many ways relentlessly mundane and often surprisingly sublime. Sitting right in the middle of the country, it is one of the flashpoints where new ideas clash with Midwest values. Hannibalians love their guns and their Bibles and their beer gardens. They also love the Mississippi and wildlife and worthy charities.

This project has been poetic archeology that digs down into the rubble to retrieve the past. It focuses on the people who lived and loved and died here. It gives voice to the men and women who populated the past. Like a forensic artist, Patricia gives us those faces and scenes through her watercolors.

HANNIBAL AT THE DOOR

Hannibal ante porte
Summer 1861

That summer day dawned bright and clear,
the humid air heating up almost immediately.
When sunrise hit that old river water
and bounced to Glascock Landing,
harbor master Jim Turner searched up and down the Mississippi
for black smoke
as boys swam and splashed off the landing,
so Jim slipped down from his perch overlooking the waterfront
to stretch his long legs for a moment only
when two alien steamboats from the north
slipped past the railroad bridge trailing white smoke
and landed without permission,
their stages set and quickly dropped with a thunderous boom,
as a whole regiment of blue coats
disembarked double-time bayonets fixed,
and the swimmers climbed out of the water mouths agape
as Jim rang his alarm bell,
and it was soon mimicked by the Fifth Street Baptist belfry;
I will always remember Professor Locke running down Main Street,
following the regiment,
waving his white arms and shouting *Hannibal ante porte,*
the old alarm cry of the Roman legions,
Hannibal ante porte,
the enemy is at the door.

ENCHANTED CONVERGENCE

The ancient ones all heard the women
singing through the thick fog
that twisted up Hannibal Creek like a rattlesnake;
the Illini and the Fox
avoided this tangled river bank
and labeled the chanters bad medicine;
Marquette and Joliet heard the high notes
through the whiteness that enveloped the river,
and then as fog lifted,
saw women dancing under the green overhanging branches
and crossed themselves three times;
Robert de La Salle ordered a landing
when he heard his angelic wilderness choir
but searched in vain all day;
the keelboat men all repeated the legend
of women in white singing on the west bank
and repeated the story around blazing campfires
to all neophytes on the keelboats;
steamboat men encountered the enchantresses
and heard them clearly from west bank to east
even above the pow pow of steam engine
and swirl of river water;
for on this very spot marked X on La Salle's map
lies an enchanted convergence of the mundane and mythical,
between Hannibal and fictional St. Petersburg,
between real Will Bowen and character Tom Sawyer,
between Uncle Dan'l and mythical Jim,
still presided over by the women in white
with their long hair blowing east in a west wind
at this landing called Hannibal,
enchanted convergence of the twain.

There and Back: Julia's Fairy Tale

Father nightly took our hands
and led us beyond sight,
beyond time,
beyond Hannibal
and back again;
Every night he pulled the curtains aside
to show us a little pig
and his house of straw,
of sticks,
and of brick;
Nightly, the story ended always
with the warning,
children, the wolf is always at the door.

Cupola

Everybody needs to climb the stairs
all the way up
to the cupola sitting on top of it all.
It is good exercise
for the body
and soul.

In the Mind's Eye

I can see it all now,
and the years fall away in the mist
as if it were yesteryear,
that old white village,
smoking and steaming on the riverbank,
whitewashed and snoring in the summer sun.
You see one place,
the town before your eyes,
but I see a village clinging to the west bank;
I see crumbling log cabins that are no longer here;
I see shadowy figures who are no longer here,
and I feel like a boy again.
I always come back,
back to Hannibal,
back to the Mississippi
if only . . .
in my mind's eye.

Samuel

The old man sits by the hearth
slowly smoking a cheap cigar,
white smoke ascending
like an ethereal tower;
His youth now captured in the books,
he sits a pale shadow of himself,
his youth bleached white in too many suns,
his hair and mustache and suit
now a Robards' white shade
by the smoking fire.

West of Eden

Somewhere in ancient memory
a ragtag band of wanderers stand mute
on the soft bank of a prehistoric river,
gazing at a flood of freshwater flowing by,
leaving abundance in its wake--
a garden of eden,
a paradise in the land between.
And the motley tribe,
brother and sister hunters and gatherers,
like plants and animals before them,
plant themselves firmly in the bottomland,
pushing roots down deep,
anchored to a place,
inventing a new word called home.
And the ancient ones handed down a legacy
to us present who mutely stand tall
on the banks of this ancient river today
in the heartland,
somewhere west of eden,
standing in the Mississippi mud,
a long way from home.

Injun Joe 1902

Joe Douglas dropped by to say he had found a young man
to take care of the horses and carriage house.
The fifteen-year-old man is a recent orphan
who is fine and trustworthy
and the son of the late Joe Bowers, one of Sam and John's bandits.
Joe D. always knows everybody and all things happening in Hannibal.
Strange how Sam's fiction turns out to be a peach of a man.

MISSISSIPPI

The town drunk snores loudly in the shade of the skids,
and there she is,
lapping against the dirt bank,
restless and moving,
dangerously alive like a monster on the loose,
hiding a secret or two on the surface
and mysteries underneath,
a tidal wave of immense proportions
pulled down river,
pulled down to Orleans,
pulled down to the gulf,
pulled down to the seven seas,
pulled down to the center of the earth,
sucking everything down
including me.

POSTCARD: EXHIBITION 1904

Dear Aunt Ella,
Wednesday last, I arranged tickets on the Quincy to St. Louis
Exhibition Train and booked two nights at the Park Hotel.
We all went down, even the servants. When we arrived at the
World Exhibition, we were all unprepared for the wonder of it
all. Forest Park is transformed. So for two days we have walked
the world from Paris to London to Berlin to an African village,
and we caught a glimpse of the big world outside Missouri and
the big future in the age to come. We rode home somewhat
subdued. Afterwards, Hannibal seemed smaller somehow.
With affection,

Nephew John

SAM CLEMENS AND THE LAST SUMMER

I remember well that last summer
when you and Sam Bowen came back unemployed pilots,
Mississippi restless and all fidgety,
with everything up in air.
Then old Absolom showed up,
and all the Hannibal boys went away for a fortnight,
and then Bull Run took up all the type,
and suddenly without warning summer was over.
Winter closed in tight,
and all the rivers froze solid,
and summer never came back again,
and so we rambled far and wide.
Sam searched the earth over,
and scoured the mining camps,
and came awfully close in the Sandwich Islands
to eternal summer in a real paradise.
He came awful close with splashing water
and a board slicing through salty waves, but not quite,
and so we mourn our loss forever,
never young and never summer ever again.
Sam tried again in Bermuda,
returning to the warmth eight times,
seeking a tonic of eternal summer,
searching for the holy grail.

JOHN ROBARDS

For me,
life was always a serious and exacting enterprise;
for me,
life demanded diligence and attention to detail
in my legal apprenticeship,
my practice,
my military service to the Confederacy,
and in the hundreds of wills and deeds and contracts
I wrote over the years
to hold the legal fabric of Hannibal, Marion County,
  and all Missouri together.
For Sam,
life was a lark,
a grand excursion
as riverboat pilot,
silver and gold miner,
newspaper reporter,
published author,
and the toast of the stage.
Somehow, some way, Sam played at life and won.

MEMO

I never thought about my own last will and testament. I have executed hundreds of them for others, but I was going to live on. I did not need one until now that I am pushing 80 years on earth, and they are all pushing me to get it done. You asked about my memorial, well, to tell truth, a plain tombstone will do for me. My true memorial is the house we built on Sixth Street. She still soars, and that is enough.

Colonel J. Robards

AFTER LAURA'S VISIT

Laura Frazier walked down Sixth Street arriving promptly at 10,
and we talked about her visit all the long way to Connecticut,
and we revisited Sam's Hartford home
over tea and cucumber sandwiches,
yet much was left on the table unsaid.
I always wondered about Laura and Sam.
Oh, I don't mean the slate days;
I mean that summer before Sam got shot
and all hell broke loose.
I always wondered about her second boy
arriving that next spring.
I always wondered, but a lady never asks
over cucumber sandwiches and tea.
Apparently, Doc Frazier never asked either.
Perhaps he wondered about a child who did not favor his father.
I always wondered,
but a lady never asks such a question.

DOLLHOUSE

Papa had Peter LeBlanc build my doll house
since he is the best cabinet maker in the whole state,
and if my little house is any indication,
why Papa is right,
and I do love it so.
Papa says I can have the big house some day
when I outgrow the little one.

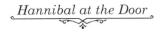

Still Birth

I built them here on the waterfront for sixteen years;
I laid the keels,
and bent the timbers in the steam press.
I watched the gilded ladies rise from keel to pilothouse
and helped gild the chimneys and decks,
and watched the carpenters work their magic
on the state rooms and grand salons.
I never missed a day.
I never tired of it all
and never regretted a damn thing
except that dark day the Fabius sank
on her maiden trip to St. Louis.
Hearing the bad news,
we all stood in stoic silence,
but our heart was breaking up on the rocks,
just like hearing that our baby girl
had been stillborn in the fog.

Hooper

Storms always call me up to the top.
to the windowed vista.
to the flash of white light and the thunderous cannonade
and driving rain mixed with hail.
The family always heads for the underground shelter
of stone basement walls,
but a butler can climb up storm ward
since a servant is somewhat expendable
in a big house like this one.

RIVER SKIFF

Hobert's boy Jim so begged me
to sail with him in that old skiff he bought from old Bill Boscht;
so we sailed up river Monday last,
up past the railroad bridge,
and past a past I had almost erased,
but remembrances long dead and buried
flew back to the *Sunshine*
tied up there that spring morn,
rocking in the current,
and baking in the blazing sun,
smoke just boiling out of her chimneys,
all repainted blue and green,
and blazoned *Intrepid* over the paddle box.
Then my levee burst under pressure
and memories came swirling down
like the Mississippi in flood stage,
and in my mind's eye I could clearly see
the *Sunshine*, an inferno on the St. Louis riverfront,
Old Sam B's ruddy face long gone these many years,
and Sam C. with ginger hair and those stupid mutton chops,
and Will B. green and strong smiling down from the Texas deck,
and the whole damned crew that last summer,
faces eager and bright with anticipation.
Now in this summer of '02,
those faces are faded white in the book,
vague on the page
of my crumbling and eroding memory.
So we floated that old skiff back down river past the icehouse
and landed vague and indefinite
on the Hannibal waterfront.

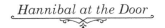

GONE FISHING

Faith is a boy
sitting on the riverbank
holding a fishing pole,
watching the line in rapt anticipation
of the giant whose fillets will feed the entire street.
Faith may permit the boy to hook the cat,
but he is ill prepared to land him;
faith alone being unable to land
a hun'ered pounder.

STORE LEDGER

One year total in the school house was enough
to master my letters,
to sign Horace Brown with a flourish,
and to read a bit of the Holy Bible,
but not enough to grasp the numbers,
and so I regard the ledger as a foreign shore I will never visit.
I can tell you how many fasteners remain in the bottom drawer,
and how many yards of calico remain on the roll,
and what I ordered from St. Louis six months ago,
but I never know if the ledger is red or black
until I am told.
I just never know.
God bless our Maggie
who stayed eight years at the schoolhouse of Mrs. Hor,
who writes a beautiful hand,
who borrows every book in town,
and who learned her ciphers well,
for without Mags
I would be a keelboat without a rudder.

They call me Mrs. Simpson in Hannibal.
That will do.
My girls call me Mattie,
and on Sundays it's quiet around here
so we all gather round the dining table,
and I am the lady of the house,
and they are my girls,
and the years fall away,
and for a moment I am Mary Ann again,
and I have choices ahead,
and I still believe that good trumps bad,
and I still know why.
Sundays bring comfort to an old non-church-going pagan
such as myself.
I have to admit I shed a tear or two
when Susie sits down at the piano and sweetly intones,
I come to the garden alone.

The regimental band played *Stars and Stripes Forever*
as Missouri boys marched down to the waterfront
and steamed off to fight the Spaniards.
Boys shouted *Remember the Maine* from the boiler deck.
Huzzah they answered from the hurricane deck,
but I remember boys in blue landing right here from Iowa
to occupy this southern town in '61.
I just want to know whose old town our Missouri boys
will occupy this old war.

MONKEY RUN

Mid night in the maelstrom
of wind and rain and hailstones the size of goose eggs,
the cyclone took them all--
the whole row of shanties
and thirty souls throttled in their sleep
by the whirlwinds.
At such a moment
grief is beyond all tears.

PREACHER MAN

I will shoot a man dead that dares call me Reverend
since it's blasphemy to say a man is revered
like God Almighty Himself.
Just call me Preacher.
Some call me hard shelled,
and maybe I am,
but there's right and there's wrong,
and there's a hell awaitin' sinners.
The good books says that God is jealously visiting iniquity
to the third and fourth generation.
I believe it's true and there's judgement to come.
I felt the call early.
The other boys would look at the clouds
to see riverboats and horses;
I always saw the angel of the Lord with a sword in his uplifted hand.
I still do.
Amen.
Praise the Lord.

BREAKFAST FOR ONE

They are all gone visiting Cousin Joe
down in St. Charles.
It's Wednesday so all the servants are off.
Hooper is still hovering around
but out and about at the moment.
Maureen came in early
and left my breakfast and the coffee pot on the dining table.
I sit alone in an empty house
silent as eternity.

SURVIVOR

I came back to Hannibal after the war
my thumb shot off
and my soul shot clean through.
The Sunday school boy came back home unrepentant,
unfit for duty,
cured of all illusions,
and a reformed Presbyterian.
I married May in the church house
for her sake,
and I treated her right,
and worshipped the ground she walked on,
and loved those babies,
but I could never go back to a church that believed
  human beings are the highest work of a loving God.
Shiloh cured me of all that nonsense
when grapeshot went clean through that old lie
and half of my regiment in the smoke
just outside a church house in Tennessee.

CLARA

Ever body calls me Cholera Clara
when I come back through on my way to Ohio,
all the others taken by the cholera,
and me alone spared,
and only 24 at the time.
Everybody gives me a wide berth,
crossing the street
and crossing themselves upon my approach,
suspecting I alone carry the sickness,
all 'cept Jane.
Oh, Lordy, I knowed all them Clemens--
John, Jane, Mela, Orion, Benjamin,
and that devil Samuel,
and sweet little Henry,
but Jane, the Mama, be a saint.
'Cause she takes me in,
makes me feel like somebody 'gain.
She even lets these ol' choleric hands
bake up some cornpone for her family.
She takes me to church as part of her family,
sits me on their pew,
and even converts this one time Methodist to Presbyterian
'cause of her.
I love Jane so
if she up and joins the Blasphemers,
I 'spect I gonna join that church too.

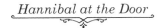

JENNY

dat wil' skinny chil' wif fire in 'is e'e
'n' da devil in 'is soul
min' me a me sometime
dat Sam chil' got gumption
oh how I loves dat chil'
we boff not much to look at
but we boff full a vinga
'n' lafta
'n' songs
'n' damn lies

BEN FRANKLIN

When his lordship disembarked at the Hannibal waterfront,
he stayed two days at the Planters Hotel before heading west
for his Grand American Hunt.
His lordship slept in the hotel
whilst his servants slept at the barn keeping an eye on the livestock,
all except the big mastiff dog
who wandered off for more than a week
and was left behind to the great distress of his lordship.
So the great big mastiff stayed with us,
just another Hannibal immigrant
among many,
but he came to rule the village
like his own canine kingdom.
We never knew his name or pedigree
so we just called him Ben Franklin
because of his uncanny resemblance to Dr. Franklin
and because he too like old Ben
had an eye for the pretty ladies.

SIMON BAUGHMAN

Oh, how the mighty have fallen.
My storied family came early to the old Dominion
and prospered in land and servants,
always in the blue book,
looking down from our great halls,
but somewhere along the line,
the poor relations headed west
to Ohio first and then beyond,
and I, aristocrat by birth and breeding,
graduate of Jefferson's University of Virginia,
educated for greatness,
ended up here
in this God-forsaken mud hole
where not one man in a hundred
knows anything about our namesake Hannibal
or the elephants he brought over the Alps.
Moreover, the rabble wouldn't give a wishbone
to hear about it.

TOM BLANKENSHIP

Not much of a drinkin' man,
I am one and out
and two if a friend offers;
so when yer ol' Pap
did not never know when to quit,
you had best figure it all out
fer yerself
'cause life is a growling bitch
for a hard drinkin' man
and his kin.

OTTO BERGHOFFER

I tell you what.
That day was the biggest shock of my life
with me standing on that old dock
halfway round the old world
in India of all places
on my grand excursion,
and who should intrude on my revels is a wonder I dare say
because here he comes sailing right by
standing on the deck of the *Suffolk*,
big as life,
and all gussied up in a white suit,
puffing white cigar smoke
like Caesar on his barge.
It was that damned Samuel L. Clemens, big as life,
he was,
and he waves big,
and I say,
What the hell are you doing here Sam?
and he up and says,
Well, I could ask you the same thing Otto.
So before I can answer,
the *Suffolk* slips away on the tide,
and Sam is gone.

CURLY

Curly is a hell of a name
for a bald man,
but Hannibalians love their ironies,
indeed they do.

JOSEPH

I was the real but unknown Indian Joe
with a Methodist education,
a year at Oberlin College,
and law clerking for Lawyer Whitlock in Cincinnati,
I was ready to slip quietly into white society
accepted as Joseph Baldwin, Esquire,
but under the skin lurked White Wolf,
son of Chief Red Hawk.
They never knew,
but I could never forget,
and so from time to time
I slip away from the law office
and sweet Allison and the children
to sleep under the stars again
and hunt alone these tame Missouri woods
like a lone wolf
and howl for Red Hawk
and utter and complete loss.

MARY BOWEN

Comin' from where I did
from those I descended from
and from the brush piles blockin' my road,
I thank the good Lord every single day
for a good strong man named Sam,
a well-built house on North Street,
two sturdy sons who made riverboat pilots,
and a sure and certain knowledge
that I am the best cook in all Hannibal.
On these facts I can rest assured.

ANDREW

At my birth Pa announced
I was to be called Andrew,
and it was so,
and God saw that it was good.
Pa instructed me to be of service always
with the expectation that I would haul water
or provide the means to feed 5000
should the occasion arise
by fetching my five loaves
and two small cat fishes.
I always did,
and God saw that all was good,
very good.

LAURA HAWKINS FRAZIER

Where on earth did his fictions come from?
I tell you the truth
it is an awful mystery to me,
and I was there from the beginning,
and he tells me I inspired his Becky,
but I just don't know . . .
Appears to be an enigma all right
for those of us
who inhabit his stories.
Oh, for heaven's sake,
I never could tell
being a black and white sort of woman,
and him being a gray sort of man.

ᏰEULAH ᎷᎯE

My first memory ever is the church house
right downtown
all plain and rustic,
log walls hand hewed,
log benches hard as rocks,
and the puncheon floor rippling underfoot like the Mississippi
with gaps between the logs,
and the hogs squealing underneath our feet,
and the preacher going on and on
into the afternoon
about one thing and another,
but somehow the spirit grabbed me early
and, after that, I never missed Sunday school
or services with prayer meeting in between,
or the ladies circle,
and brush arbor revivals,
and a thousand and one acts of service
for the One who died and is risen.
You bet I was there when we built the new church uphill
and moved from frontier logs to brick,
and so over the years my life had two parts,
succor for Ma and Pa at home
and ministering to the flock.
Dearly beloved, let us hear the conclusion to the whole matter:
Somewhere along the way, I took orders as a Presbyterian nun,
and so married to God and his church,
I had no energy or inclination
to marry a mortal man.

BARBER SHOP

We strolled down Broadway after court this afternoon
and stopped at Zeke's shop for a trim.
The topic *du jour* is Sam's approaching visit
back again to Hannibal.
I am so looking forward to seeing that old son of a bitch,
but then Preacher Norman
admits that the Fifth Street Baptist Church elders
are inviting Samuel Clemens to speak on Sunday next.
Dear God,
wonders and signs in the heavens
and in Hannibal
that I should ever see Preacher Clemens
or my name is not Colonel John Robards.

MR. AMENT

For an educated man
it's either the church,
the school,
or the press;
so I chose the newspaper business
with all its anxieties.
I freely decided to live on the edge
of a sheet of newsprint,
but perhaps,
after all,
I did some good
and informed the populous,
and started some young apprentice
on his way,
perhaps.

MOSES BATES, JR.

It is mighty hard steppin' into that long shadow
cast by an illustrious father,
always tryin' to live up to
a name like Bates,
father of Hannibal.
Seems likely to me,
Tom Blankenship had a hell of a childhood
with that old profane drunk of a father,
but Pap Blankenship's shadow was purty easy to overshadow
once Tom makes a United States Marshall out west.
We river rats know it's all about the ebb and flow,
the drought and flood,
the ups and downs,
the suns and moons,
the fathers and sons,
you know,
the ebb and flow.

PAUL MASON

When I opened the Mercantile,
the new emporium was an innovation
in the merchandise business.
Hannibal had always been a trading center,
but trade is a rough and tumble
dance out here.
Coming from Baltimore,
I was unused to the rough business etiquette
or to the standard Missouri question:
What do you get for something like this?
Obviously, indirection is a west bank art form
more honored in the breach than in the observance.

SALLIE

two days shine clear in ma min'
that ol' rainy day Mr John bought me off'n ol' Boggs
'n' den dat sunny day at Bowen's Barn
dat I got sold to Mr. Claude
res' of dem long days all runs t'getha 'til freedom come
leas' dey calls it freedom
de hours all de same t'ing
washin'
cleanin' never change
but if n de roof ov'head mine
'n' food in de cu'bard mine
I b'long to m'self now
so I keeps workin' 'n' hopin'
dat de real freedom come
one des days

SADIE

I was 17 when July and me walks across the river ice
and lands on the Hannibal waterfront,
me strong as a horse
'n' July sickly;
good thing we wintered near Doc Meredith,
otherwise, July 'ould never made it;
so dreams of Californi' died that winter,
and we stayed on
where a sickly man
might not roll logs for a livin',
but could still roll cigars
and make a livin'.
The good Lord rolls in mysterious ways,
don't he?

EVELYN

Dear Samuel,
On your visit back to our fair city in 1855
we talked about *As You Like It,*
you and I.
You had seen the play in New Orleans,
and you were all aglow with theater dust in your ginger hair.
Do you remember?
I had seen the play in Springfield and was much amazed.
Young and all bright-eyed and bushy tailed,
we reveled in the magic.
Do you remember Sam?
Now, I sit here in my Fifth Street parlor
exiled from the Duke's court,
no longer reveling.
My revels are all ended Sam.
Are yours?
I remember when we danced alone
in Hannibal's Forest of Arden,
we called it.
It was our bucolic rendezvous,
our place of exile where all things were possible,
but now the old park is no place for the old,
since forced exile can be a cold, cold place
on the west bank.
With fond remembrances,
Evelyn

RIVER WIDOW

A dove in the cherry tree calls softly
coo,
coo,
to her mate in the apple tree in the village below
and down to the river
and up to the stars;
a candle in the front window burns precariously
flicker,
flicker,
flickering down Cardiff Hill to the village below
and down to the river
and up to the stars;
captain latches a door behind him quietly
click,
click,
and walks down the hill that ordinary day
and continues down to the river
looking up at the stars;
May last the Mississippi was flooding violently
swish,
swish,
against the weak levee
and rising up Cardiff Hill from the river
and threatening to flood the stars;
a strong current swirls menacingly
too strong,
too strong,
down river all the way to St. Louis
and on to New Orleans
and beyond the stars;
a kiss and a wink bestowed customarily
too soon,
too soon,
as he smiled down on the village

and on his way down river
and all the way up to the stars;
this May day was all so ordinary, but the current was savagely
wrong,
wrong,
down past Glascock Island
and past the chain of rocks
and up to the stars;
a candle in the window burns sadly
out,
out,
sending darkness down the hill
and down to the river
and up to the starlight above;
a widow sits in a window alone, all burned out completely
so blue,
so blue,
looking for answers down in the village
and down on the river
and up in the stars.

POLECAT

The Fourth Street boys always called me Polecat
'cause of the smell,
more like a stench that gets under your skin
and will not let go
even with vigorous application of lye soap.
When a boy starts work at the hog butchery at 12,
Polecat is a purty good handle
to hang yer hat on.
All in all,
Polecat suits me.

MARGARET TOBIN

Da always said I was tough as nails,
and when push came to shove,
I suppose I was,
tough enough at least
to ride that wild mustang mare
called Colorado
before she was broke.

FIONA

I'll tell you a truth
ye can trust
'til yer dyin' day,
love's a curse;
I loved himself
from the first sight of him,
but a servant, indentured as I am,
and stationed as I am,
can do nothin' but watch;
the voice inside me silenced,
the life inside me frozen
'til such a day that I am free
to move on my own,
to speak my own voice,
but 'til then,
I will watch
and dream
and hope
my time will come
one day.

HARBOR MASTER JIM

The powers that be
hired me to straighten out Glascock Landing
since it were a tangled mess
with too many boats in those steamboat years
before war came to the old Mississippi;
for at its crest
that old river current were bringing us
over 400 landings a week average,
and I kept it all right as rain
with one very loud mouth,
one long poling stick,
and one fine and delicate use of exquisite profanity;
preacher says all of us gets our talents from God
and we must not hide ours;
I utter truth when I tell you
that I could never hide my talents under a bushel.

MOLLY'S DREAM

Curious and restless
with a hankerin' for life,
I left Hannibal behind,
hopin' to see some of the wide world,
hopin' to drive a stake into ground
on a claim of my own,
hopin' to find the leprechaun's pot a gold;
Da always said that gold was true
as Joseph, Mary, and the Christ child hisself;
Da was right,
and Mr. Brown found that pot of gold
under a Colorado rainbow.

TULIPS

Green fingertips push up through the soil
straining to touch April sunlight,
time travelers from a Victorian past,
rooted deep in Hannibal soil,
opening green to the warmth,
and infusing another April morning
with the first bloom.

STEFAN

I came along first to work in the cement plant
and live in the dormitory
while I saved every penny to send for Lizabet and the girls.
So and, now we have a company house in Ilasco
and new Hungarian neighbors from Budapest
living down at the end of the street
in case I want to speak magyar.
End of the work day
I come home to a little piece of Hungary
on the West Bank
and paprikas kroumple on the hot stove,
and as I wash up on the back stoop,
I smile, oh, how I smile.
After mass Sundays,
Lizabet's cabbage rolls are hatalmas bírságot
as the American's say,
mighty fine,
Yes sir,
mighty fine indeed.
Yes sir, as American as cabbage rolls,
baseball,
and apple pie.

THE MIDNIGHT CRY

It was Tuesday
at the time appointed
at the hour foretold in ancient times
by the prophet Daniel and John the revelator;
so on that appointed day all the Hannibal advent flock
climbed up to the top of Lover's Leap
to await the second coming of Jesus Christ
in the clouds as the holy Bible foretold
and that was in '44;
that day dawned, and we arrived at the summit
with nigh on a hundred souls in tow,
singing and praising God and staring east,
but by supper time we retained only a handful;
some huddled in the dark,
crying above the village
as if their hearts would crack under the strain of it all,
certain of certain certainties but under awful stress,
staying 'til midnight struck like a funeral dirge,
the air full of mourning shrouds,
and then stumbling down the trail,
all the sorrowful way home those fifty years ago;
we survivors remember that midnight cry
with the certainty of a child's faith
and the memory of what shattered that day;
today the three remaining mourners
climb back up,
slower on this October 22, 1894 ascent,
fifty years late,
to eat our picnic in silence,
the wind sweeping the trees bare

on the cool October summit,
and we button our coats up high,
and brace against the autumn winds,
still waiting,
still searching an overcast sky
for a small cloud in the east.

Sam's Letter to John Robards

My Dear Friend John,
Your kind invitation to the hospitality
of your Hannibal home
made me smile.
At moments like this,
we are boys again
forging friendships to last a lifetime.
Still a river pirate at heart,
I promise to be on my best behavior
so none of your Sixth Street neighbors
shall have cause to call the law.
Yourself, a respected member of the bar
has to be somewhat careful
when harboring fugitives these days.
Too many hotels in my life
weary the body and soul
and make your kindness truly a balm in Gilead.
These days, I am just a tattered old sloop
listing to starboard
and looking for safe harborage.
Your Friend Always,
Samuel L. Clemens

DREAM GIRLS

When I was young and foolish,
my little sister and me would sit on the front porch nights
looking up at the stars
and out to the Mississippi that lapped at our front gate,
and we watched the steamboats heading out
and dreamed we would marry a rich man one day
who would take us to exotic places like Memphis
or New Orleans or maybe even Cincinnati,
and we would wear fine gowns
and go to theater in a black carriage
pulled by a matching pair of high steppers
and live in a fine house.
I foolishly shared my dream with my mother one day
who laughed at my pitiful girl dreams
and reminded me
if wishes were horses then beggars would ride.
These days, I dream of that old front porch
and the wide Mississippi
and wish that I could go back and sit again with my sister.
That dream would be so much better
than all the hogs bellies in ol' Cincinnati.

OPPORTUNITY KNOCKIN'

Us boys apprenticed and unpaid and hungry
for all that cash money can buy,
talked big about headin' down to the Brazils
or headin' out to Californi'
money to be made.
And we dreamed of all that money
in coffee beans just ready to be plucked off'n
coffee plants we would grow,
but the ol' war ended speculations
and other schemes,
and some of us couldn't pass up the glory
of a stint in hell
courtesy of ol' General Sterling Price out west;
as they say,
when it comes to schemes and dreams,
you win some,
and boys,
you lose some.

CONFEDERACY

Somehow,
in the fullness of time,
when we all aligned our compasses to true north
and pigheadedly headed south
on the Mississippi
to join up,
somehow,
we had a gut feeling
this would prove to be
one colossal boondoggle.

ICEMAN

My handle is James P. Phelps,
but everybody in town just calls me Iceman
since I always carry an ice pick in my belt
and pump ice water through my veins.
The wife says my hands and feet
always feel cold as ice;
stands to reason
since I spend all that time in the ice house,
winters sawing out the big blocks
and packing them in sawdust,
summers hauling blocks out to the steamboats headin' south,
precious gift from the cold season,
making mint juleps possible in ol' New Orleans
and giving the wife cold feet
in the bed nights.

NAOMI BATES

Moses always looked down the river
and saw around the river bend,
no, no, not a carnival act,
mind you,
but the future of glowing prosperity
of industry, agriculture, and enterprise,
building a civil dream
out of the harsh wilderness reality,
but somehow, he needed my assurance
that he was on the right path
to the future.

Moses Bates

I am not the Moses who led the children
out of Egypt;
I am the Moses who led some children
to a muddy riverbank
and named it for Hannibal Creek on the south end of our survey
and platted out a new town in the year of our Lord 1819,
hard on the heels of Mr. Lewis and Mr. Clark
and the purchase of Louisiana.
Today the papers report ol' Tom Jefferson
still alive and kicking at Monticello,
founding his new university around a rotunda of his design,
and ol' John Adams still drawing breath
and reliving all his struggles for independence
in the corridors of his fading memory.
And closer home, General Clark down in St. Louis
still governs the Missouri Territory,
and I am here on the riverbank,
Moses in the wilderness,
surveying the promise land.

Cynic

Mrs. Horr taught us well;
oh, I don't mean just letters and ciphers,
but what she called axioms.
Now, all these years later,
it all comes to mind
in quiet moments of solitude.
I believe politicians when they are not talking
'cause Mrs. Horr always said
actions always speak louder than words.

ERV GOINGS

Cool days of fall mean hog killin' to me
and ever since I was up to my Daddy's belt buckle,
I helped out;
our days full of hog squealing,
murderous axe blows thudding home,
slippery, bloody ground under foot,
and the smell of dressing out,
sausage making,
and boiling down to lard
never leaving nostrils even in a hard wind.
The stench of it all stays on and on,
but we killed to eat.
Man killin' is a heap bigger mess
with thunderous cannon fire,
massed volleys throwing up smoke smelling of cordite
and the air of death
and the screaming
and the pleading calls for water,
and the smell of it all
and the memory stays on and on,
but we killed to win;
most times the kills just left
to rot on the ground,
and sometimes a skull peeks
back out at the world through a shallow grave;
in any case
seems like such a waste
since nobody was killin' to eat
in that ol' man killin'.

SEMPER AD ASTRA

January of '33 sure starts as a portentous month
from the beginning
with various and sundry signs and wonders in the heavens,
and on earth
those strange hoof prints in the waterfront mud
that May and June as the river floods,
certainly not deer or moose or bison the hunters assert,
but large striding biped hoof prints
like a man on the run.
Then early morning in October searching for runaway mules
cross Bear Creek,
he stands next to a sweet gum,
horns and all,
fearless, staring right at me
with those goat eyes
so I run in terror,
but then late night on November 12
with church bells ringing alarm
the whole village turns out to see stars
falling precipitously overhead like November rain
all night until first light,
and then to top it all,
December 5,
I take shelter from freezing rain in that old dry cave
back side of Cardiff Hill
when a whole tribe of hairy, biped beasts
with their curved horns and musky smell
converge on my shelter jabbering loudly to one another
in their own unknown tongue,
clacking their hooves on the stone floor,
even the young ones playing loud, boisterous tag
as I curl tighter and tighter behind a large rock quaking in my boots,
they start a fire

and act like parishioners at a Baptist potluck after Sunday service,
jawing on until dawn when they leave one by one.
So I make my way back over the hill
to a town I hardly recognize to share my tale
and show some of the reddish fur from off the cave floor,
but I am tarred and feathered by laughter,
mocked and maligned something fierce,
and exiled to Quincy forever
for the crime of bald faced fabrication.

Deacon Harpeth

One time or t'other all kinds of men of the cloth hit this here town,
witch doctors and shamans all painted under the feathers,
Jesuit priests holding a brass cross high overhead,
Methodist circuit riders with a voice of thunderation,
Baptists with a whole wide river of baptizing water before them,
and steamboat preachers who conjure up a collar
somewhere between Louisiana and Hannibal.
The righteous ones did much good in this untamed land;
the quacks and charlatans
devised schemes to leave town
with heavier carpet bags than they arrived with all.
We even had our brush arbor camp meetings
and that Gospel Steamboat Revival
with the brass band and puppet show.
Of course, the whole town turned out for the festivities
with little to rival such an entertainment.
All in all, my experience tells me that in religion,
I must always observe with a wary eye and some misgivings
since the servants of the good Lord
are mightly prone to wander off the straight and narrow path,
salvation bein' hard for a man of the cloth to hang onto.

BOGEY MAN

When I would rouse from nightmares
to see him outside my window peering in,
I always screamed bloody murder,
and Ma always appeared at the door
to soothe and insist I go back to the land of Nod;
Ma always hugged me
and asserted that the man at the window
was only my imagination playing tricks on me,
but on her deathbed
she finally confessed
that he was real all along,
and that I should watch out.

SMITTY

I tell you
I have no earthly idea
how many iron shoes I pounded out over the years
or how many wagon and buggy wheels I finished off
pounding a red hot iron ring onto the wheel
and dousing it with cold water
to shrink the metal tight
or how many iron nails I made.
I only know the ringing in my ears never ceases
even on Sundays,
and the thunderous sledge wakes me oft from a deep sleep,
and the crash of metal against metal
is like a small aftershock
after the New Madrid quake.

CLARABELLE COUGHLIN

James is older'n me
by some twenty five year,
bachelor farming 3500 acres of cotton at New Madrid
with 20 mules and 30 servants
until the quakes shook most everything loose
and made dirt ripples ten foot high across the acres,
and wrecked the land something fierce,
running off the mules and chickens
and scattering the servants to the high weeds
and putting James Coughlin
out of the plantation business.
So James gets a land grant
and on his way out of New Madrid,
he stops off at my Daddy's place
to make me a bonifide offer of marriage,
and so, land grant in hand,
we land in Hannibal
to unload the remaining six mules and four servants
to prosper in the dry goods business on Main Street,
to settle in for the duration
and eventually,
over time,
for me to fall in love with sweet James,
the best man I could ever know.

Richard Garey

Arthur and Prudence

Love is a strange and mysterious malady
spread about by who knows what,
perhaps a microbe borne on the night air;
in any case I was afflicted
from the first time I laid eyes on Prudence
skipping down 3rd Street,
her bright curls peeking out from under her bonnet,
and her green dress festooned with white ribbons,
her upturned face wearing a smile,
her laughter ringing down to Main Street,
but she never saw me looking back,
never imagined my affliction
as I watched her grow up,
attended her wedding to Jim in the First Presbyterian Church,
observed as she mothered four children
and became a lady of the town
before their immigration west,
before cholera took her Jim and all her grown children
out there in Kansas.
So she came back sick and destitute
and dependent on the kindness of strangers,
and so, I took her in
and provided for her to the bitter end
and loved her
and cared for her
just as I always had,
never once making my confession.

KING FISCHER AND SHEBA'S EGYPTIAN TONIC

Every springtime me and my pretty mulatto gal
hit Hannibal with spring tonic for all;
Sheba sings in her blue dress and matching blue hat,
all groomed out like a real lady;
I play the banjo and crowds gather like migrating fowl to wetlands,
and we always sell out our stock;
We claim its good for fevers, gouts, liver spots, and cancers,
cures them all, least that's what Sheba sings too;
Sheba's Egyptian Tonic straight from Cairo, elixir of the Pharaoh,
even known on occasion to raise the recent dead.
Of course, we make it with corn whiskey and spices down in Alton,
but the real curative always has been and still is faith;
And every spring Sheba and I sell a little faith and corn whiskey
in a glass bottle of Sheba's Egyptian Tonic.

MAURICE GIRARDEAU

You say that you are Americain
and somehow something new
on the horizon,
but you are only Anglais at heart,
plundering your way across the continent,
rolling to the Pacific and beyond.
I hear the words manifest destiny bandied about,
like this is something new and shiny,
but I think manifest destiny is just old time piracy.
La France has seen this all before,
but as a Frenchman,
I am not bitter.

MRS. SHELBY BIGGER

The curse of the pretty girl fell on me early;
Shelby was a doe pursued by hounds
until one of the dirty dogs caught me
and up and left town
and left me with child
but without visible means of support;
it was not a good fix to be in,
but Granny said I always had gumption,
so knowing Harold Bigger always had eyes for me,
I got all gussied up
and marched right into his bank on Broadway,
right in front of all those people,
and demanded he do the right thing by me,
being with child and all,
and so, Harold up and marries me on the spot,
pretty much lifting the pretty girl curse single-handedly
and landing me in a big house up on Sixth Street for good.

HOBART WYATT

When a master bourbon maker from Kentucky
lands on the Hannibal waterfront
to offload his still and barrels from the *Alton,*
we all take note
and salute the pilot who brought him.
When a master bourbon maker
with skill unmatched up river and down,
lands to set up shop on the west bank,
well, then, publicans have to shout,
the Lord be praised!

AUNT PHOEBE 1871

I landed on the west bank from a world turned upside down,
from a time when we were subjects of the Crown,
born British in 1771,
I was 10 when it was all over,
and we were our own.
Being from Philadelphia,
I saw it all--
delegates to the Congress,
Mr. Jefferson strolling by our house each morning,
hands behind his back,
his mind far away,
Mr. John Adams, his short legs trotting along,
always late for an appointment,
his hands full of papers.
Mr. Hamilton always dressed smartly for the occasion,
his eyes flashing confidence,
Mr. Hancock in a carriage with footmen
waving at me from his window,
General Washington's ragtag army shuffling through town,
followed in short order by the redcoats all smart and fearsome,
their drums booming and trumpets blaring.
Yes children, I lived through the redcoat invasions
and that old uncivil war
and flood and pestilence
and the house afire that burned us out and sent us west
with the new country
and brought me here to the west bank.
Now in '71,
I am 100 and soon heading for harvest home
at any moment,
in the twinkling of an eye
when the last trumpet shall sound,
I shall land home.
Glory! Glory! Hallelujah!

CORNELIA WESSER

Yesterday, I emptied Grandma Jessup's old trunk
and unpacked a lot of memories
at the bottom of which was that old sash
they placed around my neck that July 4 in '59.
Mayor Sims named 15-year-old me Miss Liberty,
and that's what it still proclaims
from the bottom of the truck,
prettiest girl in Hannibal.
That was all before Gerald's itch to homestead in Nebraska,
that was before the cyclones and grass fires,
and those dark clouds of locust,
and the monster blizzards with snow to the roofline,
and that infernal wind blowing dust into every crevice,
and clothes never truly clean,
and food never free of the grit.
And so I looked back at the shine
of Grandma's old scratched mirror today
and did not recognize the face shining back,
all dried out and cracked.
Gerald says being busted we can't move a thing.
I say it is just as well
to leave it all,
memories and all,
and start over with no illusions,
fresh and unencumbered by the past.

GERALD WESSER

Hannibal boys before the war
grew up lookin' west
and up to the older boys
like Ab Grimes
and Will Bowen
and Sam Bowen, Jr.
and Sam Clemens,
all young success stories,
all riverboat pilots,
and all envied by all,
and so I dreamed of something beyond Hannibal,
something to call my own,
a piece of ground to be mine
in seven years of frontier homesteading.
Cornelia and me found that piece of ground
in northwest Nebraska
and we also found more than we bargained for,
and I failed her.
Not able to keep my promises to Cornelia,
we went bust after five years,
the mules dead in their traces,
the chickens cleaned out by hawks and coyotes,
the crop blackened by a raging firestorm
we barely escaped in our cellar.
And so we head back home,
wore out and plumb down and out
and all busted up.

ℬEAUREGARD ℒONG

When I started out,
it was just about a simple pine box.
That was it.
Now they all want the extras
like stain and varnish
and brass fittings.
Don't they know frills won't last
more 'n a year or two?
So nowadays,
I deal in memorials for overhead
just for show.
I hate to admit it,
but memorials don't do much good either
when your time comes.
But, oh Lordy, Lordy,
I visited Bellefontaine Cemetery down in St. Louis last fall,
and some of them city people
spend more on a mausoleum
than I did on my whole house on South Fifth Street.
I am afraid that when my time comes,
I would rather rest at the bottom of the old Mississippi
'cause that old river would be quite a memorial overhead
if I do say so myself.

MEMORY

Today, my aged recollections
are vague and somewhat untrustworthy,
but I do recollect moonlight on river water
and a silver skiff slipping through silver eddies.
I believe I do remember
silver plated catfish
flashing mirrored light
on a silver fishing line
and a campfire's rosy glow on Glascock Island
and wood smoke ascending
white in the calm
and the smoky musk of frying catfish
mixed up with Mississippi island perfume
and young silver bodies
in the moonlight,
silver droplets cascading back
down arms and chins,
resplendent in the summer of it all
if I do remember any of it
at all.

WILLY

I learned early
but really too late to make much of a difference
that when a boy and a locomotive at the switching yard
are on a collision course,
the locomotive always wins.
So to this day I drag my bum leg with joy
'cause I coulda lost a whole lot more
that ol' day.

GEORGE MCNAIRY

For a free Negro like me
slavery was a faraway thing growing up,
something whispered about amongst the freemen
in New Philadelphia.
Oh, I saw the runaways
wild with hunger and fright
and helped them on their way to Chicago
and helped Free Frank build the town
and got my education in the school house sound.
But the times, they came around,
as they always do,
and it was time in '62 to put on the blue
and fight like a free man,
and so I fought for three years
for that flag with stars and stripes
and came out alive,
but just barely,
with a scar or two
and a big dream for a Negro.
When the railroad bypassed New Philadelphia,
I moved Beulah and the girls
and my store
over to Hannibal
and built my business right at the tip of the wedge,
right there on Broadway,
and prospered as a free man
and always flew that old flag
off the side of my Broadway dream.

PENELOPE SNOW

Landon Simpson Snow
loved me gracing his arm,
light and ethereal
on the dance floor,
cultured and fashionable on his arm,
the epitome of grace,
but Landon never loved me,
the real me,
the woman of flesh and blood,
never once asking who I was
or why on earth
I took his old arm
in the first place.

KATIE KERRY

It ain't that hard being one of Sadie's girls,
and it just ain't that much about passion and such;
it ain't nothing about bein' the prettiest girl in town;
it's just about lending a listening ear
to a man who has nobody left
to hear him anymore;
so I listen like a priest
and sometimes grant absolution
in my own way;
providing solace in a lonely world
as the only humanity some men can touch;
so for a Catholic girl like me
a cathouse can be mighty close
to the confessional.
Ain't that a hell of a thing?

CORBIN'S STRING

Me and Jefferson know a thing or two
about traveling horseback.
Comin' out here from Carolina,
we learned the hard way
that you need a horse to ride
and a string of animals to spare.
I had even painted California or Bust
on my saddlebags
when we landed in Hannibal
off the ferry
and rested here a few days
when I was snagged by May Belle Culver
and changed my status to
Busted in Hannibal
by a red-headed gal woman.

SAM BOWEN AT BOWEN'S LIVERY

Eventually everybody comes to my barn
on Dead Man's Alley,
but they always come needing something,
a horse to be shoed,
a buggy wheel to be trued
a livery for their livestock.
Horses and mules are easy enough
and are content with a stall
and some hay and a little corn,
but men,
oh, now that is another matter,
men always want more,
always more,
never content with just room and board.

CHIEF COOK AND BOTTLE WASHER

I rolled in here
on the mail packet back in '59
like a beached wreck,
out of all luck,
but with some idea how to roast and bake and fry
from my New Orleans days.
Old Pritchard at Old Planters
says if I want my supper tonight
I had best cook it myself
since the damned cook up and quit,
and so I did,
and I been here ever since,
still pleasing most
but offending the New Englanders
with too much Cajun spice.
Preacher Prescott claims my food
is downright sinful
and that food should be plain
and unadorned.
I say I think God must have a big appetite himself
and perhaps he's Cajun
or at least a Presbyterian who likes crayfish.

ꙶHE ᴘARRᴏꙶ ꙶOUSE

Mary and me
like to walk on over to the Captain's house
on Third Street
for the Friday evening show.
Customarily, if it don't rain,
a small assemblage faces that ol' bird
Capt. Moore picked up somewheres along the way
in a card game.
It's always a hoot
when that colorful and literate fowl
whistles at Mary,
and cusses at me,
and then the crowd roars.
You can hear that parrot whistle
all the way over to Broadway,
and you can hear that parrot squeak,
you god-damned son of a bitch,
all the way down to Main,
and you can hear the crowd hoot and holler
all the way up to Sixth Street,
and you can hear that bird shout,
you infernal sons of Belzebub,
all over town.

JENNIE

That woman at the carnival
with her head all tied up
in that silk rag
looked into my eyes
and at my calloused hands
before announcing to the carnival crowd
that the fault was in my stars.
Well, my stars,
when I gaze at the stars of a clear night,
they all look just about perfect to me
and without fault
in my eyes.
That's just about the way
Jennifer McAlexander sees it.
If anybody here
is to blame,
if there is fault
to be laid,
that would be me
and not my stars.

IF

If for nothing else,
every body needs a cupola up on top;
if for nothing else,
it gives one a little perspective.

At McDowell's Candy Store

I wish to God I had had the foresight
to place some of Gertrude McDowell's gum drops
in one of Dr. Meredith's medicine jars
and had sealed it all up with paraffin,
defying time.
What a treat it would have been
for an old man to break that seal
and taste the sweetness of youth again,
to savor the sweet tang of life
preserved in a glass jar!
But, sorry to say,
Herb Ostermier's youth
was about devouring gum drops
on the spot,
overstuffing his mouth,
inhaling sweetness like it was endless,
never mind tomorrow.
It never crossed my mind
to save up some sweetness
for a tasteless day
so as to be able suck the nectar from a gum drop
at the end of days.

Doc Meredith

So many,
yes, so many,
their faces rising in my dreams,
pleading for that which I cannot give,
but like the apostles of old
I practice the laying on of hands
and dispense words,
optimistic and bright as a spring morn.
My patients see me as mythic
holding the talisman of medusa,
raising the brass serpent on my staff,
encouraging all to look and live.
I see myself as a medicine man without balm,
fraudulent and unapprenticed in the trade.
However, sometimes a tonic will do
and sometimes loving hands and bright words
still conjure up a miracle.

My Father's House

Independence is just a word
until you earn it,
and I never did.
I, Haywood Baughman,
took my Father's money
and supposedly worked for his railroad
but never lay a mile of my own track
and never made any of it my rolling stock
and wasted the sum of my days
and never became president myself,
and so I end up here
at the end my life,
living safe and sound
where I started out
and dying a slow death
in my Father's house.

Room

These plaster walls and woodwork
hold many stories,
embrace many secrets,
remember many guests
past and present,
famous and anonymous.
These plaster walls and woodwork
are still a stage on which many scenes
are played out dramatic and comedic;
these solid doors and painted woodwork
wait patiently for the next playwright.

CATFISH

Every single night of my life
I set my lines as I have always done
since I was nine years of age,
and my Pa up and drownded,
and left me to fend for myself,
and every mornin' I fill the canoe with fish
when it's not floodin'.
Then Glascock Landing becomes my fish emporium,
and by the time seven bells ring
from the Baptist belfrey,
I am sold out,
except for the best uns
that's saved for myself
to be breaded in cornmeal and fried and e't
with cornpone
and Irish taters
and cold buttermilk
all gobbled up with great relish.
I never been to the schoolhouse,
but I been to school on the river,
and I watched that old river bring the big catfish everything he need,
just pushes life his way.
So Mississippi brings me all I needs
since I is the big, old Hannibal catfish
waitin' under the railroad bridge.

SANDY

They took us from the Eastern Shore of the old blue hen
and trucked us all to Annapolis
after old Master Holbein died in '45
and everything went up for sale to the highest bidder,
and so they sold me away from my Mammy at that auction,
just nine years of age and on my own
when they loaded us onto a ship called the *Roselinde*
with my hands in child shackles,
and we sailed on the morning tide for New Orleans
where I was sold to slave traders heading up the Mississippi
and on to St. Louis chained on the boiler deck
of the side wheeler *Louisiana*.
Again in St. Louis I was sold to Mr. Claude of Byrd Street,
and then Jane Clemens rented me in '47
growing up with Sam and Henry and the other town boys.
Now it all seems so long ago that I live a free man in Iowa
and go by the name Sanderson Clemens.

JOHNNY PUCINI

I come to Hannibal all the way from Rome
to work in the cement plant,
after all, Rome invented the cement business
2000 years ago,
and I work there for five years,
but now I want to start my own business
as a plumber.
I see opportunity in 1895,
I see a bright future for me in plumbing,
after all,
my Rome also start this thing
called indoor plumbing.

HANNIBAL JAILHOUSE CONFESSION

Murder is not such a bad word
when one comes to the clear understanding
that some men deserve killing.
Above the law and given over
to such crimes and felonies
that would make a real lady blush
but never summoned to the bar to answer,
the guilty party went on with his crimes.
Justice called out to me
to avenge the blood of the innocent,
to act for the defenseless,
and so I go to my hanging tomorrow
for killing Horace Brownlow
but shriven for my sins by heavenly father
and ready to meet justice
knowing I have set it all to right
and defended those who could not defend themselves
and acted above the law
as a member of the tribe of Dan.

NED

A horse is a horse as horses go, they say,
but not Ned with that extra sparkle in his eyes,
with that extra snap to his gait,
with that extra pedigree
that added class to any old buggy.
As horses go,
I shall miss him very much.

BERNARDO

A boy sold to the circus by his own father
must earn his own keep early
any way he can,
feeding the animals
and mucking out
and doing whatever others do not want to do.
Apprenticed to the animal trainer,
I wrangled bears and lions
on and off steamboats and into arenas for six long years
until the night the *Lafayette* sank,
and I made my dash for freedom
across the Mississippi on the back of Rocky,
the trained grizzly bear and old friend,
and we both landed cold and wet
but alive and free at last
on the west bank.

SOLOMON HASS

When I left for Cuba,
the photo shows a hard drinkin',
hard whiskey brawlin',
all night dancin' Hannibal hell-raiser.
It weren't long 'til they shipped me back
to the south side
shot up by the Spaniards
and sucked dry by the yellow fever,
a livin' skeleton, I was,
so I never once fought again,
and I never once danced again,
not to say I didn't ever want to.

RUDOLF AND CLARA

The truth is,
for me, San Francisco has been good.
Here on the Bay I have prospered
and grown old,
seen California fill up with immigrants,
seen manifest destiny unfold
like that old flag with the bear on it,
but I tell you,
truth be told,
I never wanted to leave Hannibal,
and Mississippi River mud still pumps
through my veins.
All along, it was Clara
had the itch to lay claim to a plot
in the golden land,
and she did.
We struggled in here in '56,
all worn to frazzles,
the livestock dead,
and us stumbling over those mountains
just ahead of the snows.
We made it,
but Clara was too far gone.
She made it to the land of gold
but just barely.
She did not stay long,
just long enough to stake her claim
to a small plot on a Frisco hill
where the stone slab is inscribed,
Clara Hawkins Rest in Peace.

ALIAS

I arrived on the west bank
with little more than the shirt on my back
and a burning ambition
and a knack for faro,
but I never used my real name
or told about my war crimes in western Missouri.
I got me a stake at the tables
and then my own place
and made me some money
since everybody in Hannibal is a gambler
or they wouldn't be here in the first place.
One night, I killed a man right here at my bar
when he called me cheat
and drew down first,
and if you look close at the floorboards,
the bloodstain remains ghostlike and indistinct.
Jeb Smallwood drew down first is true
so no charges were ever filed.
Today I stand accused
only by the bloodstain on the floorboards
and the memory of my other bloody crimes.

STORY TELLER

Uncle Dan'l made sure we knew
that everybody has a story to tell,
even the animals.
Most are unsung;
most float on the breeze
for a moment only
like a bird song;
most are ethereal like wood smoke
in a west wind,
soon gone and soon forgotten,
but every once in a great while,
a story gets set in lead type,
and the ink gets pressed onto the page,
and the pages get blown to the four winds.
Every once in a while a tale gets told and retold,
printed and reprinted,
until it grows bigger than life itself
and takes its place on Mt. Olympus
with all the other immortals
like *Huckleberry Finn.*

Star Skiff

Sometimes Fred fetches me at the witchin' hour
an' we borrow an ol' skiff
from the landin'
and let her run down the current,
us layin' on our backs lookin' up and out,
dizzy with staring at that ol' river of stars they call Milky Way,
so afraid of floatin' away ourselves,
we grab the gunnels with both hands
holding on tight
just in case we might fall up and out.
I just wonder if some other pilgrim
might just be floatin'
a star current somewhere,
lookin' up and out at our speck of dust
in this sea of stars,
afraid he too might just float
up and away.
I wonder.

SIRENS ON THE RIVER BANK

When the founders settled on the classical name
of that old Carthaginian,
they made sure nobody hereabouts
could ever forget the alarm,
the call to arms,
the terror of mythological elephants
disembarking on our western shore,
clambering over our molehills,
stampeding toward the open door
while river sirens,
long hair streaming,
lounge on the riverbank singing in falsetto,
seducing us to madness,
singing *Hannibal ante porte. . .*
enemies is at the door,
and every single time the sirens wail
we are seduced to melodic alarm
and sing our own version of the river song
as we drift happily toward the unseen snags
lying just below the surface,
mesmerized by the song,
sedated into inaction,
and doomed to our own destruction.
Hannibal ante porte
the sopranos still sing.

ℬIO ℛICHARD 𝒢AREY

W riter/Actor/Educator featured on CBS Sunday Morning and NPR All Things Considered.

Richard Garey is a resident of Samuel Clemens' world. He has lived in historic Hannibal for fifteen years and is connected to its past and present. The emotional background for Hannibal at the Door came from research into Sam Clemens early life on the Mississippi River and the historic buildings Garey has restored in Hannibal including the Planters Barn Theater 1849, the Parrot House 1861, and the Robards Mansion 1871.

Richard is a stage actor and performs Mark Twain Himself live in Hannibal each season and continues to develop other original theater productions. He has performed his original, one-man shows in over 40 states in theaters, on university campuses, and for churches. He has taught theater and literature, appeared in television commercials, and written seven plays. Richard holds a Masters in English from James Madison University in Virginia.

www.heritagestage.com • rgarey@hotmail.com

....

Patricia Garey's art may be seen at the Mississippi River Gallery in Hannibal or on line at **www.patriciagarey.com.**

....

Skye Childers is a freelance designer and layout artist. He can be contacted at **Skye.Childers@gmail.com.**

CPSIA information can be obtained
at www.ICGtesting.com
Printed in the USA
FSHW01n1518190818
51505FS